THE GREATEST SOCCER L'EGENDS

THRILLING ANECDOTES, ASTONISHING FACTS, AND UNFORGETTABLE SUCCESS STORIES OF THE GAME'S BIGGEST STARS. FULLY ILLUSTRATED IN COLOR.

ROOKIELAND

ROOKIELAND

At RookieLand, we believe every child has the potential to become a champion.

Our stories bring to life the incredible journeys of famous athletes, alongside inspiring tales of imaginary heroes, to spark a passion for sports in young readers.

Whether it's scoring the winning goal, running the fastest lap, or simply celebrating teamwork and perseverance, our stories inspire the next generation of athletes.

We created each RookieLand book with the belief that dreams can come true through dedication, creativity, and heart.

To keep the inspiration, growth, and fun going even after you have finished the book, we've prepared some special **BONUSES** for you:

- 50+ Printable Coloring Pages: ignite creativity and fun while keeping young minds active and inspired.
- 3 Sneak Peeks of Other RookieLand Books: discover new adventures and the inspiring stories of more athletes.
- Parenting Tips: practical advice to support your child's journey in sports and in life.
- Fun Family Recipes and Activities: take part in activities that promote family bonding and a healthy lifestyle.
- Exclusive Facebook Group: join and take part in giveaways to win more fantastic books.

Scan the QR CODE below to access these gifts and receive exclusive previews of our upcoming releases. It only takes a few seconds!

PLAYER VALUE
$33M

NATIONALITY
ARG

JUNE 24, 1987
37 YEARS

HEIGHT
5'54"

PREFERRED FOOT
LEFT

STRENGTHS
LONG-RANGE SHOT
PENALTY TAKER
DEEP-LYING PLAYMAKER

SKILL MOVES
☆☆☆☆☆

WEAK FOOT
☆☆☆☆☆

WEAKNESSES
DEFENSIVE CONTRIBUTION

JERSEY NO.
10

LIONEL MESSI
90

PAC 80		DRI 94	
SHO 87		DEF 33	
PAS 90		PHY 64	

TRANSFER HISTORY AND MARKET VALUE

71M — BARCELONA 2021

35M — PARIS SAINT GERMAN 2023

30M — INTER MIAMI 2024

POSITION

LIONEL MESSI

THE LITTLE STAR WHO BECAME A HERO

From an early age, Leo knew that soccer was his destiny. He raced across the field, dribbling past everyone, always keeping the ball glued to his foot.

He wasn't as big or strong as other children, but he had a huge dream. The ball seemed like a part of him something he controlled like magic.

At age 11, however, Leo discovered that he had a condition that prevented him from growing like other kids. It seemed that his dream was slipping away. But Leo didn't give up. Together with his family, he began treatment with courage and determination.

One day, scouts from the club Barcelona saw him playing and immediately knew he was special. They brought him to Spain, where Leo began training in Barcelona's famous academy, La Masia.

Even though he was small, he had incredible drive and talent. His teammates called him "The Flea."

Leo began to shine, scoring spectacular goals and dribbling past everyone. He quickly became a star for Barcelona and one of the world's top players. In 2012, he scored an impressive 91 goals in a season, breaking an old record. In 2017, he scored his 500th goal against Real Madrid, securing a victory for Barcelona.

Besides being a great soccer player, Leo is also a generous person. He helps those in need and never forgets his origins. He has won many championships and cups with Barcelona, but his biggest dream was to win a World Cup with Argentina.

In 2022, in Qatar, that dream came true. Leo led Argentina to victory in the World Cup, scoring decisive goals and becoming a national hero. At last, his greatest dream was fulfilled, cementing his status as a living soccer legend.

LIONEL MESSI

MESSI'S ACCOMPLISHMENTS

Messi has won the Ballon d'Or, the award recognizing the best footballer in the world, a record eight times! No other player has won so many Ballon d'Or awards.

He has scored over 800 goals during his career and holds the record for the most goals scored with a single team, netting 672 goals for Barcelona.

Messi led Argentina to victory in the 2022 FIFA World Cup, scoring seven goals during the tournament, including two in the final.

In Spanish La Liga, Messi holds the record for the most goals (474), assists (192), and hat tricks (36). He is the all-time top scorer and assist leader in the Spanish league!

He has won 43 trophies in his career, including the 2021 Copa America and 10 La Liga championships with Barcelona.

LIONEL MESSI
CLASH OF TITANS

Imagine the two best soccer players in the world, the ones who have won the most Ballon d'Or awards: Messi and Ronaldo. One day, they finally faced each other in a highly anticipated match.

It was 2009, and the setting was the iconic Olympic Stadium in Rome. On one side was Ronaldo's Manchester United, the defending champions full of stars. On the other was Messi's Barcelona, a team that played soccer like a perfect machine.

Coached by Guardiola, Barcelona had Messi, his number 10, who worked magic on the field.

The match ended 2–0 in favor of Barcelona. One of the most unforgettable moments was when Messi scored a header goal that remained etched in everyone's memory.

That year, Messi won everything with Barcelona: La Liga, the Copa del Rey, the Champions League, the UEFA Super Cup, the Spanish Super Cup, and the Club World Cup. Barcelona became the first club to win six trophies in one year!

Thanks to Messi, who scored 38 goals in all competitions, he won his first Golden Shoe and also his first Ballon d'Or, becoming the best player in the world at only 22 years old.

ANEDDOTI SU MESSI

LIONEL MESSI

Did you know that Leo Messi has Italian roots? His great-great-grandfather, Angelo Messi, left Italy in 1893 to live in Argentina!

Messi has a famous celebration where he points both hands toward the sky. This gesture is a tribute to his grandmother, Celia, who played a crucial role in nurturing his love for soccer.

Did you know that Leo is one of the highest-paid soccer players of all time? He reportedly earns as much as $54 million a year! With all the trophies he has won, he truly deserves it.

Messi's passion for Yerba Mate comes from his childhood in Argentina, where he enjoyed this traditional drink with family and friends. Today, like many Argentines, he cannot do without it, keeping this cultural tradition alive.

Did you know that a jewelry store in Japan made a gold sculpture of Messi's left foot? It was valued at millions of dollars and was auctioned off for charity after an earthquake in Japan.

PLAYER VALUE
$196M

NATIONALITY
NOR 🇳🇴

JULY 21, 2000
23 YEARS

HEIGHT
6'36"

PREFERRED FOOT
LEFT

STRENGTHS
FINISHING
PENALTY TAKER
POSITIONING SENSE

SKILL MOVES
★★★☆☆

WEAK FOOT
★★★☆☆

WEAKNESSES
DEFENSIVE CONTRIBUTION

JERSEY NO.
9

ERLING HAALAND
91

PAC 89	DRI 80
SHO 93	DEF 45
PAS 66	PHY 88

TRANSFER HISTORY AND MARKET VALUE

- **5M** MOLDE *2018*
- **45M** RB LEIPZIG *2019*
- **150M** B.DORTMUND *2022*
- **180M** MAN CITY *2023*

POSITION

ST

ERLING HAALAND
THE YOUNG FORWARD

Erling Haaland has become a great soccer champion. From an early age, he dreamed of a brilliant career in the world's greatest stadiums and he succeeded.

Erling was born in Leeds, England, in 2000. His dad, AlfInge Haaland, played for Leeds United, a famous soccer team. However, one day his father suffered a severe knee injury and had to stop playing soccer. This was a very difficult time for the whole family, but Erling found the strength to continue.

He also began playing soccer, quickly showcasing his talent. It didn't matter that he was younger than the others, the smallest in his school, because he was great at scoring goals! He always played with such passion and was not afraid to face opponents who were bigger than him.

Erling began his career as a forward when he joined the main team at Bryne, a club in cold and snowy Norway, at only 15 years old. Even though he was so young, his talent was undeniable. He improved every day, and his performances started gaining widespread attention.

Erling then moved to Austria to play for Red Bull Salzburg, where he continued to score incredible goals. His outstanding performance caught the eye of Borussia Dortmund, a top team in Germany. With Dortmund, Erling continued to amaze everyone with his strength and speed.

ERLING HAALAND

HAALAND'S ACCOMPLISHMENTS

Erling Haaland has achieved remarkable feats in the Champions League. He scored three goals in his first game against Genk and scored two goals in four consecutive games. Most impressively, he scored five goals against Leipzig, making him one of the top scorers in Champions League history.

He has scored 41 goals in 38 Champions League games by the age of just 23 years old. He is already 17th on the all-time scoring list, surpassing great players like Eto'o, Griezmann, Kaka, and Rooney. He is now tied with Agüero and is closing in on Del Piero and Neymar.

Erling Haaland is so quick at scoring goals that he has set numerous records! He became the youngest player to score 20 goals in the Champions League, achieving this feat at just 20 years and 231 days old.

In the UEFA Champions League round of 16 second leg in the 2022/23 season against Leipzig, Haaland scored an astonishing five goals by himself.

Haaland is highly skilled with both feet! He scored 28 goals with his left foot, nine with his right foot, and four with headers.

ERLING HAALAND
A PERFECT DEBUT

Haaland made his UEFA Champions League debut in a round of 16 match while playing for Borussia Dortmund against Paris Saint-Germain.

Erling Haaland did something truly remarkable in that game. His team won 2–1, thanks to the incredible goals he scored on his own.

That day was very important for Erling Haaland. He showed everyone just how talented he is, even in such a prestigious competition as the Champions League. From that moment on, everyone knew that he was destined to become one of the best soccer players in the world.

CURIOSITIES ABOUT HAALAND

ERLING HAALAND

Erling Haaland was a champion even as a child! He set the record for the highest jump for his age, reaching an impressive 1.63 meters. He was only five years old at the time!

To match his height, you would need to stack 194 Mickey Mouse comics! Erling Haaland is 6'4 ft tall.

Haaland scored nine goals in a single game during the Under-20 World Cup against Honduras. It was an extraordinary feat that included three hat tricks in that match.

Haaland loves soccer so much that he once said he sleeps with five soccer balls!

Erling Haaland is so fast that he could compete with top athletes in a race! He once ran 60 meters in just 6.64 seconds. The fastest athletes in the world complete the same distance in only 6.34 seconds!

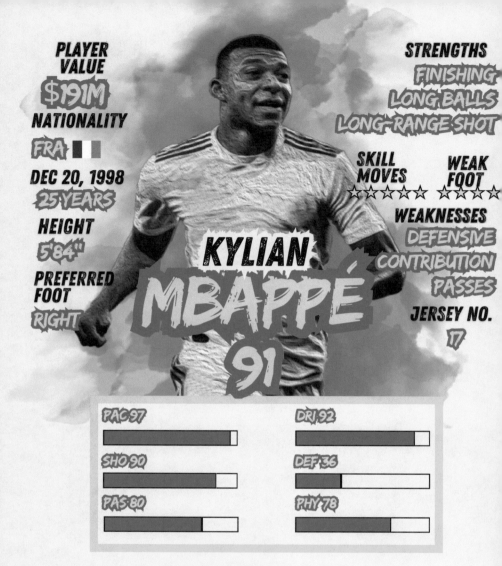

PLAYER VALUE
$191M

NATIONALITY
FRA

DEC 20, 1998
25 YEARS

HEIGHT
5'84"

PREFERRED FOOT
RIGHT

KYLIAN MBAPPÉ
91

STRENGTHS
FINISHING
LONG BALLS
LONG-RANGE SHOT

SKILL MOVES
☆☆☆☆☆

WEAK FOOT
☆☆☆☆

WEAKNESSES
DEFENSIVE CONTRIBUTION
PASSES

JERSEY NO.
17

PAC 97
DRI 92
SHO 90
DEF 36
PAS 80
PHY 78

TRANSFER HISTORY AND MARKET VALUE

35M — MONACO 2017
180M — PSG 2023
180M — REAL MADRID 2024

POSITION

KYLIAN MBAPPÉ

THE PATH TO SUCCESS

Have you ever heard of a little boy who slept with a soccer ball next to his bed and watched countless games on TV? That was Kylian!

Mbappé, wearing the number 10 jersey of the French national team, grew up in a family of athletes in the town of Bondy, France. From a very young age, he loved playing soccer, and his family always supported him.

His parents, Fayza and Wilfred Mbappé, were his first fans, and his two brothers, Jires and Ethan, played with him every day. His father, Wilfried, who was also his coach, taught him all the best moves and motivated him to always give his best.

But Kylian did not only love soccer; he also had a secret passion for music! He attended a conservatory where he learned to play the flute and to sing. He was such a talented and versatile boy!

His journey in soccer began with the local team, AS Bondy, where he impressed everyone with his dribbling skills and his incredible speed. Just imagine he can run so fast that he reaches 38 kilometers per hour in just 30 meters!

Scouts from Stade Rennais, a major team, noticed his talent and offered him the opportunity to become a professional player.

Kylian continued to grow and improve until he was selected to train at Clairefontaine, the prestigious academy where young talents learned to become soccer stars.

He started playing for AS Monaco, where he scored his first professional goal at just 17 years old! Since then, he has become one of the strongest and most skilled players in the world.

Today, he also plays for the French national team. In this excellent squad, he won the World Cup. There, he met great champions and attracted the attention of famous clubs such as Chelsea and Real Madrid, one of the most renowned teams in the world. He now wears the number 9 jersey for Real Madrid! Whenever he steps onto the field, everyone watches him in admiration, captivated by his amazing moves and extraordinary talent.

Kylian is not only a soccer champion but also a generous person with a strong desire to help others. He has donated a lot of money to charity and has used his talent and generosity to assist many people. Kylian Mbappé is a true role model for all children who love soccer and dream of becoming champions one day. Who knows? Maybe you, too, could one day play on the most famous fields in the world!

KYLIAN MBAPPÉ

MBAPPÉ'S ACCOMPLISHMENTS

During the World Cup final, Kylian Mbappé did something incredible: he scored a goal that helped France become world champions in 2018!

Kylian Mbappé played his first game for AS Monaco, becoming the youngest ever to do so for the club. He was only 16 years old.

Did you know he was the youngest player to score a goal in World Cup history? He was just 19 years old when it happened.

In 2018, Mbappé won the Kopa Trophy, a special award for the best young soccer player under the age of 21. This award, given by France Football magazine, is named after the famous French footballer Raymond Kopa.

In the 2022 World Cup, Mbappé scored eight goals, including a hat trick in the final! Although France did not win, it was an incredible tournament for him, and he proved to everyone that he is one of the best soccer players in the world!

KYLIAN MBAPPÉ
A YOUNG PRODIGY

In 2018, the soccer world witnessed the birth of a new star: Kylian Mbappé. At just 19 years old, with his magical plays and incredible goals, he led France to win the World Cup title in Russia.

Mbappé was already a promising talent, but at the World Cup, he stunned everyone. He was like lightning on the field, impossible to stop. He scored no fewer than four goals, one against Argentina and a decisive one in the final against Croatia.

His speed, technique, and flair for goal have made him a true national hero. Mbappé has made French fans dream and has won the admiration of the entire world.

It was as if he were living a dream that became reality not only because of his extraordinary talent, but also because of his commitment and passion. With hard work and tenacity, even the most ambitious goals can be achieved.

ANECDOTES ABOUT MBAPPÉ

 Although many people think Cristiano Ronaldo was his first idol, Kylian Mbappé actually first admired Zinédine Zidane for all he accomplished with the French national team.

The Real Madrid star has loved sneakers and soccer boots since he was a child. His favorites were Nike Vapors, and today he even has a dedicated section on the Nike website where he sells his favorite shoes!

 Do you know that he is faster than Usain Bolt? Yes, he is! Kylian Mbappé is so fast that he once ran faster than Usain Bolt, the world-famous Jamaican sprinter.

Although he was born in France, Kylian Mbappé could have played for Algeria or Cameroon due to his parents' origins.

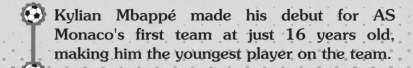 Kylian Mbappé made his debut for AS Monaco's first team at just 16 years old, making him the youngest player on the team.

CRISTIANO RONALDO

89

PLAYER VALUE
$15.6M

NATIONALITY
POR

FEB 5, 1985
39 YEARS

HEIGHT
6'14"

PREFERRED FOOT
RIGHT

STRENGTHS
PENALTY TAKER
GAME MANAGEMENT
HIGH PRESSING

SKILL MOVES
☆☆☆☆☆

WEAK FOOT
☆☆☆☆☆

WEAKNESSES
DEFENSIVE CONTRIBUTION
PASSES

JERSEY NO.
7

PAC 77	DRI 80
SHO 88	DEF 34
PAS 75	PHY 74

TRANSFER HISTORY AND MARKET VALUE

Value	Club	Year
18M	SPORTING LISBOA	2004
60M	MAN UTD	2008
100M	REAL MADRID	2018
45M	JUVENTUS	2021
20M	MAN UTD	2022
15M	AL-NASSR	2024

POSITION

ST

CRISTIANO RONALDO

FROM A HUMBLE FAMILY TO STADIUMS AROUND THE WORLD

Cristiano Ronaldo was born in Madeira, Portugal, and from a young age, he loved playing soccer. Although his family was not wealthy, Cristiano was determined to become a great soccer player.

He played soccer every day, even when he was supposed to be doing homework or when it was raining outside. He loved the game so much that he sometimes skipped family events just to play.

At 14, he made the bold decision to quit school to focus entirely on his soccer training. Although his parents were initially hesitant, Cristiano knew deep inside that he could become a soccer star.

His coaches quickly recognized his immense talent and did everything they could to place him on strong teams. However, one day, his dream of becoming a soccer player was threatened by a heart condition, which forced Ronaldo to take a break for treatment. After a successful operation, he returned to the field more determined than ever.

At just 18 years old, he began playing for Manchester United after being noticed by the team members, who urged their coach to bring Cristiano into the club.

With Manchester United, Cristiano won the Champions League and the Premier League. He scored numerous goals and earned his first Ballon d'Or.

After his time with Manchester United, Cristiano moved to Real Madrid, where he continued to win trophies and break records. He later played for Juventus in Italy and then returned to Manchester United, continuing to be one of the best soccer players in the world.

Cristiano is not only a great soccer player but also a generous person. He helps many people through his charity work and strives to make the world a better place for his children, not only for his own children but for all children.

CRISTIANO RONALDO
RONALDO'S ACCOMPLISHMENTS

In 2018, while playing for Real Madrid, Ronaldo scored an incredible goal against Juventus in the Champions League quarterfinals. He jumped very high and, in an acrobatic move called a bicycle kick, struck the ball with his feet while it was in the air, sending it into the corner of the net. This goal was so spectacular that even the Juventus fans stood up to applaud him.

Cristiano Ronaldo played an extraordinary game in the 2017 UEFA Champions League final in Cardiff, Wales. Ronaldo scored two goals during the match, contributing decisively to Real Madrid's 4–1 victory over Juventus. His first goal came in the 20th minute with a powerful shot from inside the box, and the second goal came in the 64th minute with a precise header off a Luka Modric cross. This goal marked his 600th career goal and made Ronaldo the first player to score in three different Champions League finals.

In 2016, Ronaldo led Portugal to victory in the European Championship, one of the most prestigious tournaments for national teams in Europe. In the final against France, Ronaldo was injured early and had to leave the field in tears. However, he continued to encourage his teammates from the bench, and in the end, Portugal won 1–0. Although he couldn't play much of the final, his fighting spirit and leadership were crucial to the team's success.

Ronaldo has scored 140 goals in the Champions League, more than any other player. The Champions League is the most prestigious competition for soccer clubs in Europe, and to score so many goals in this competition is an incredible achievement.

Ronaldo has scored 130 goals for Portugal, more than any other player in the history of men's soccer.

During his time at Real Madrid, Ronaldo scored 450 goals in 438 games, making him the club's all-time leading scorer.

CRISTIANO RONALDO

CHAMPIONS' TOP SCORER

In 2008, Cristiano was only 23 years old, but he was already thrilling fans whenever he stepped onto the field. He was an extraordinary forward, capable of scoring incredible goals. And that night, against Chelsea, he did something truly special.

The game was intense, with both teams fighting hard. Suddenly, Ronaldo found himself in the right place at the right time. His teammate, Wes Brown, sent a perfect cross, and Cristiano soared through the air like a kite, heading the ball into the net. The crowd erupted with joy!

But Chelsea didn't give up easily. They equalized, and the match went to penalty kicks.
Ronaldo approached the ball with confidence, ready to score. He struck it powerfully, but the opposing goalkeeper made an incredible save! Everyone held their breath.

All was not lost, as soccer is full of twists and turns. Chelsea had a chance to win but missed the decisive shot. After four rounds of penalties, Manchester United emerged victorious!

That night, Cristiano Ronaldo became the best player in Europe, winning the Golden Shoe for his fantastic goals and the Ballon d'Or for being the best player in the world!

CRISTIANO RONALDO

Cristiano Ronaldo was the first Portuguese to play for Manchester United. Initially, he wore the number 28 jersey, the same number he had at Sporting Lisbon. Although his favorite number was 7, he felt it was too big a responsibility to take on that number, which had been worn by great players like Eric Cantona and David Beckham.

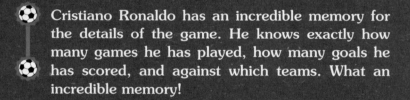

Ronaldo is not only a great soccer player but also very generous. He donated one of his Golden Shoes, won in 2011, to raise 1.5 million euros to fund schools for children in Gaza, showing his big heart.

Cristiano Ronaldo has an incredible memory for the details of the game. He knows exactly how many games he has played, how many goals he has scored, and against which teams. What an incredible memory!

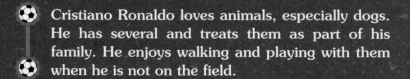

He was the first soccer player to score more than 100 goals in the history of the Champions League.

Cristiano Ronaldo loves animals, especially dogs. He has several and treats them as part of his family. He enjoys walking and playing with them when he is not on the field.

PLAYER VALUE
$52M

NATIONALITY
BEL ▮▮

JUNE 28, 1991
33 YEARS

HEIGHT
5'94"

STRENGTHS
CONTINUITY
DEEP-LYING PLAYMAKER
HIGH PRESSING

SKILL MOVES
☆☆☆☆☆

WEAK FOOT
☆☆☆☆☆

WEAKNESSES
DEFENSIVE CONTRIBUTION
DUELS

KEVIN
DE BRUYNE
91

PREFERRED FOOT
RIGHT

JERSEY NO.
17

PAC 72		DRI 87	
SHO 88		DEF 66	
PAS 94		PHY 78	

TRANSFER HISTORY AND MARKET VALUE

9M GENK 2012
10M WENDER BREMEN 2013
15M CHELSEA 2014
45M WOLFSBURG 2015
50M MAN CITY 2024

POSITION

KEVIN DE BRUYNE

THE SOCCER PLAYER WHO NEVER LOSES THE BALL

From an early age, De Bruyne showed a special talent for soccer. Born in Belgium, he started playing soccer in his hometown of Drongen when he was only four years old. His skills were so remarkable that by the age of 15, he was signed by a major team, Genk. But life isn't always easy, even for future superstars like Kevin.

At 15, Kevin had to leave his family and move far away to pursue his soccer career. It was a difficult time, but his strength and determination saw him through. He worked hard and continued to improve his game.

After Genk, Kevin played for other top teams, including Werder Bremen, Wolfsburg, Chelsea, and Manchester City. At Manchester City, he was instrumental in winning five Premier League titles, dominating the English league for several seasons. His success didn't stop there; De Bruyne also lifted two FA Community Shields, five English League Cups, the prestigious UEFA Champions League in 2023, the UEFA Super Cup, and the FIFA Club World Cup.

Kevin also plays for his country, Belgium. Since 2010, he has been one of the stars of the Belgian national team. In 2018, he helped his team secure third place in the World Cup, a fantastic achievement.

But Kevin is not only just a great soccer player; he is also a loving husband and father. He has a beautiful family and cherishes the time he spends with them when he is not on the pitch.

KEVIN DE BRUYNE

DE BRUYNE'S ACCOMPLISHMENTS

In 2013, while playing for Werder Bremen in the Bundesliga, Kevin De Bruyne scored a wonderful goal in a crucial game against Eintracht Frankfurt. This goal helped Werder Bremen avoid relegation, keeping them in the top tier of German soccer.

In 2015, during his time with Wolfsburg, Kevin was extraordinary, making 19 assists in a single Bundesliga season an impressive feat that highlighted his exceptional playmaking abilities

In a crucial Champions League quarterfinal match against PSG, Kevin scored a goal that helped Manchester City advance to the semifinals for the first time in the club's history.

In the 2020 Champions League match between Manchester City and Real Madrid, Kevin scored a perfect penalty, enabling Manchester City to progress to the next stage of the competition.

In a Premier League clash between Manchester City and Chelsea, Kevin scored a fantastic goal that secured a victory for his team, bringing them closer to winning the league title.

KEVIN DE BRUYNE

THE KING OF ASSISTS

After a challenging period at Chelsea under Jose Mourinho, Kevin decided to return to Germany, where he had previously played for Werder Bremen. He joined Wolfsburg, and there he thrived, achieving excellent results.

While he scored amazing goals, what stood out even more was his ability to provide assists to his teammates.

In one season, Kevin broke the Bundesliga record for assists, which had been held by Zvjezdan Misimovic. He managed to make 19 assists, a number never before seen in the league!

His performances were met with widespread admiration. Fans adored him, and his teammates nicknamed him "the Assist King." Kevin's record remained unbeaten for five years until another superstar, Thomas Müller, surpassed it with 21 assists.

Even though Müller eventually broke his record, Kevin's achievement will always be a magical moment in his career, a testament to his incredible talent and his ability to entertain and inspire with his soccer skills.

ANECDOTES ABOUT DE BRUYNE

KEVIN DE BRUYNE

Kevin De Bruyne was born in Belgium, but his mother is originally from Burundi, Africa. This means he could have also played soccer for Burundi's national team.

Kevin co-authored a book called Keep It Simple, where he shares the story of how he became so good at playing soccer.

The young soccer star is multilingual, speaking Dutch, English, French, and German! This helps him communicate easily with players and fans from all over the world.

Kevin has a foundation that helps impoverished children, demonstrating his commitment to giving back to the community.

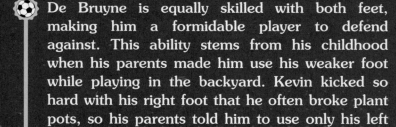

De Bruyne is equally skilled with both feet, making him a formidable player to defend against. This ability stems from his childhood when his parents made him use his weaker foot while playing in the backyard. Kevin kicked so hard with his right foot that he often broke plant pots, so his parents told him to use only his left foot.

PLAYER VALUE
$170M

NATIONALITY
ENG

JUNE 29, 2003
21 YEARS

HEIGHT
6'17"

PREFERRED FOOT
RIGHT

STRENGTHS
HIGH PRESSING
LONG BALLS

SKILL MOVES
☆☆☆☆

WEAK FOOT
☆☆☆☆

WEAKNESSES
AERIAL DUELS

JERSEY NO.
5

JUDE
BELLINGHAM
86

PAC 76   DRI 85
SHO 75   DEF 78
PAS 79   PHY 82

TRANSFER HISTORY AND MARKET VALUE

11M   BIRMINGHAM CITY   2020
120M   B. DORTMUND   2023
180M   REAL MADRID 2024

POSITION

AM
CM

JUDE BELLINGHAM

A LITTLE BOY WITH SOCCER IN HIS HEART

Jude grew up in a small English town with his family., harboring a big dream: to play soccer. From an early age, he kicked the ball everywhere he went in the garden, at school, and even inside the house (much to his mother's occasional dismay!). He was exceptionally talented, and everyone who saw him play knew he had something special.

At just eight years old, Jude joined the Birmingham City youth team. He was the smallest and the most fragile, but also the most talented. He trained hard every day with dedication and passion.

Despite the challenges and obstacles he faced, Jude never gave up. At the age of 15, Jude became the youngest player to make his debut with the Birmingham City first team. He was a child prodigy, and soon everyone was talking about him. Major teams from across Europe wanted him, but Jude chose to stay at Birmingham for another year to help his team grow.

The following year, at age 16, Jude scored his first professional goal. It was August 31, 2019, and Birmingham faced Stoke City at home. Jude, who came on as a substitute for Kyle Hurst in the 60th minute, scored the decisive goal in the 74th minute, securing victory for his team.

At 17, Jude made a difficult decision: he left his beloved Birmingham City to play for Borussia Dortmund, one of the biggest teams in Europe. It was a significant leap, but Jude was ready. In Germany, Jude began playing as an attacking midfielder, a more offensive role than the central midfielder he played at Birmingham.

He competed in the German Bundesliga, one of the most challenging and prestigious leagues in Europe. Then, at age 19, he played in the Champions League, winning the title with Real Madrid.

JUDE BELLINGHAM

BELLINGHAM'S ACCOMPLISHMENTS

During a match between Real Madrid and Getafe on September 2, 2023, Bellingham scored the winning goal for Real Madrid in the 94th minute with a close-range shot from a Lucas Vazquez cross. This goal secured a crucial victory for the team and highlighted Bellingham's knack for decisive plays.

In April 2024, Real Madrid faced Barcelona in a thrilling match. Barcelona was leading 1–0 with only minutes left, but Bellingham didn't give up! In the 87th minute, he scored a stunning long-range goal to equalize the game. Then, in the 92nd minute, he scored again from close range, giving Real Madrid the victory! Thanks to him, his team moved closer to winning the La Liga championship.

During a Champions League match in 2023 between Real Madrid and Union Berlin, the game was tied at 0–0 in the 80th minute. Bellingham received the ball and took an incredible shot from a long distance, sending the ball straight into the net. Real Madrid won 2–0, thanks to his decisive goal.

In 2022, Borussia Dortmund played Eintracht Frankfurt. Dortmund was losing 2–1, with only a few minutes left. In the 87th minute, Bellingham took a shot that was deflected into the net, tying the game 2–2. This goal earned Dortmund a crucial point in the title race.

When Bellingham was just 16 years old, he played for Birmingham City against Stoke City. In the 76th minute, with the game at 1–0 to Stoke, Bellingham took a shot that was deflected into the goal, making him the youngest scorer in the club's history!

JUDE BELLINGHAM

THE EUROPEAN CHAMPIONSHIPS 2024

The stands at the Veltins-Arena in Gelsenkirchen, Germany, were packed with screaming fans. The tension was palpable as England trailed 1–0 to Slovakia in the European Championships. The team was on the brink of elimination, with their championship dream slipping away.

In the fifth minute of stoppage time, when hope seemed lost, Jude launched himself into a spectacular bicycle kick. The ball rocketed into the net, making it 1–1. The game was saved!

The stadium erupted with joy. Jude ran to the camera and winked at all the children watching from home. He had saved England, who went on to win the game in overtime and advance to the quarterfinals.

JUDE BELLINGHA

Jude has a younger brother, Jobe, who also plays soccer. They have a lot of fun together and often practice in the backyard!

The English footballer was the youngest Borussia Dortmund player to score a goal.

He greatly admired two legendary champions, Wayne Rooney and Steven Gerrard. He owns their jerseys and strives to play like them every time he steps onto the field.

Jude made his debut for the England national team at just 17 years old, making him one of the youngest players ever to do so.

When Jude played for Birmingham City, he wore the number 22. In honor of his contributions, Birmingham City retired the number 22 jersey when he moved to Borussia Dortmund, ensuring no other player would wear the same number as Bellingham.

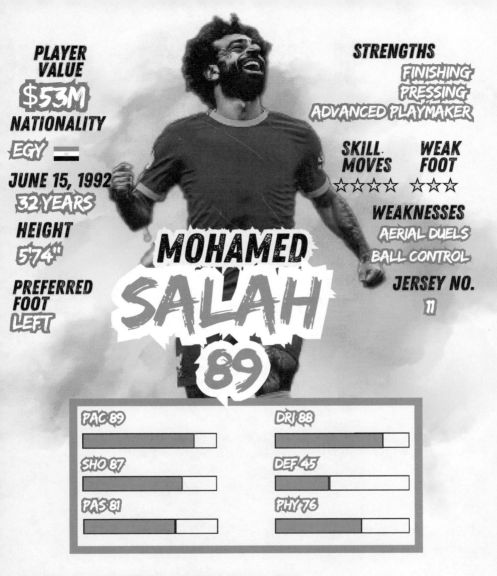

MOHAMED SALAH
89

PLAYER VALUE
$53M

NATIONALITY
EGY

JUNE 15, 1992
32 YEARS

HEIGHT
5'74"

PREFERRED FOOT
LEFT

STRENGTHS
FINISHING
PRESSING
ADVANCED PLAYMAKER

SKILL MOVES
☆☆☆☆☆

WEAK FOOT
☆☆☆

WEAKNESSES
AERIAL DUELS
BALL CONTROL

JERSEY NO.
11

PAC 89

DRI 88

SHO 87

DEF 45

PAS 81

PHY 76

TRANSFER HISTORY AND MARKET VALUE

1,5M AL-MOKAWLOON 2012
8,50M BASEL 2013
12M CHELSEA 2014
13M FIORENTINA 2015
35M ROMA 2017
55M LIVERPOOL 2024

POSITION

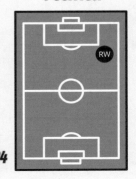

RW

MOHAMED SALAH

THE GREAT MO WHO CONQUERED STADIUMS AROUND THE WORLD

Mohamed Salah discovered his passion for soccer at a very young age. He would watch his idols Ronaldo, Zidane, and Totti on TV and then go out with his friends to try to imitate their moves.

At just 14 years old, Salah signed his first contract with Arab Contractors. The club was far from his home, so he had to endure long daily commutes, often spending hours on buses and changing multiple times to reach the training ground. But once he arrived, it was as if the journey hadn't tired him at all he would chase the ball with the speed of lightning.

His talent did not go unnoticed. After stints with Basel in Switzerland and Chelsea in England, he joined Fiorentina in Italy, where he made a big impression before moving to AS Roma.

With the Giallorossi, Salah scored 15 goals in one season, dazzling everyone with his dribbling skills and speed.

But it was with Liverpool that Salah truly made history. His move in 2017 quickly led to success, including winning the Champions League in 2019, where he scored one of the fastest goals in the history of the competition's final. He became the first Egyptian to win the Premier League Golden Boot and continued to impress with outstanding performances, earning the title of African Player of the Year multiple times.

Salah also played a pivotal role in the Egyptian national team.

He scored crucial goals in World Cup qualifiers and participated in the African Cup of Nations, proudly representing his country in international tournaments.

In addition to his achievements on the field, Mohamed Salah is admired for his humility and dedication to family and community. He is a living example of how talent, determination, and hard work can turn a dream into reality, inspiring millions of young soccer players around the world.

MOHAMED SALAH
SALAH'S ACCOMPLISHMENTS

In March 2018, Liverpool faced Watford at Anfield, where Mohamed Salah scored four, contributing significantly to Liverpool's 5–0 victory. It was one of Salah's most memorable performances during his record-breaking season with Liverpool.

In September 2018, Salah won the Puskás Award for a stunning goal in the Merseyside derby against Everton. The spectacular shot flew past the opposing goalkeeper, contributing to Liverpool's victory and earning global praise as one of the best goals of the year.

During his first season with Liverpool, Salah scored 32 Premier League goals, his best season ever. In the 2023/24 season, he scored 18 goals in the league.

On January 19, 2020, in a Premier League match between Liverpool and Manchester United at Anfield, Salah scored a decisive goal in the 90th minute after a perfect long throw from goalkeeper Alisson Becker. Salah calmly ran forward with the ball and scored past Manchester United's goalkeeper David de Gea, securing victory for Liverpool.

Salah won the PFA Fans' Player of the Year award in the Premier League for the 2020–21 season. During that season, he scored 22 goals and provided 5 assists in the league.

MOHAMED SALAH

SALAH LEADS LIVERPOOL TO VICTORY

It was June 1, 2019, in Madrid, Spain, and Mohamed Salah stood at the penalty spot with the ball at his feet. He was wearing Liverpool's red jersey, playing the most important game of his career: the Champions League final against another English team, Tottenham Hotspur. Liverpool was already leading 1–0.

With great calm and concentration, Salah kicked the ball toward the opponent's goal. The Tottenham goalkeeper dived desperately, but the ball sailed straight into the net! Liverpool scored, and the whole stadium erupted with joy.

But the game was not over yet. Tottenham tried hard to recover, but Salah and his teammates defended their lead and won 2–0, becoming European champions!

It was a moment of triumph, happiness, and pride for everyone who supports this incredible team. On that day, Salah not only scored an important goal but also etched his name in soccer history. Every match has the potential to become legendary, just like that magical night in Madrid with Mohamed Salah and Liverpool.

ANECDOTES ABOUT SALAH

MOHAMED SALAH

 Did you know that Mohamed Salah's dad was a great lover of soccer? He was a coach and taught Mohamed how to play soccer from an early age! Much of what Salah can do with the ball is thanks to his father.

 When Salah scores a goal, he kneels down to thank God. It is his special prayer to show his gratitude for his achievements.

Once, a thief broke into Salah's family home. Instead of getting angry, Salah spoke with the police to help the thief find a job! The thief became very grateful to Salah for giving him a second chance.

Do you know what Salah's favorite food is? It is called kushari, a delicious dish made with rice, noodles, lentils, and various other ingredients! Whenever he returns to Egypt, Salah always makes sure to enjoy this traditional dish.

 Salah became the fastest player in Liverpool's history to score 50 goals for the club, reaching this milestone quicker than anyone before him.

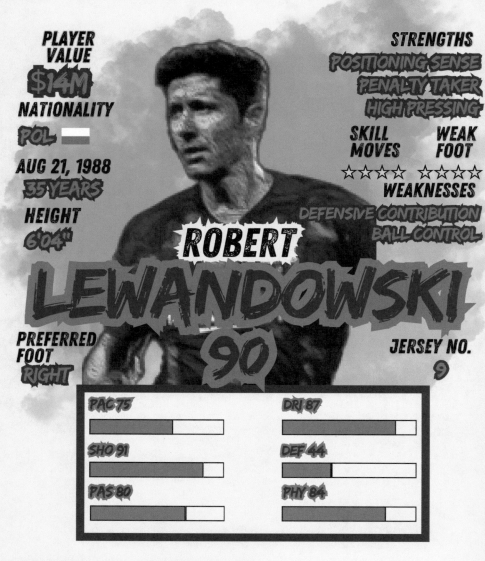

PLAYER VALUE
$14M

NATIONALITY
POL

AUG 21, 1988
35 YEARS

HEIGHT
6'04"

STRENGTHS
POSITIONING SENSE
PENALTY TAKER
HIGH PRESSING

SKILL MOVES
☆☆☆☆☆

WEAK FOOT
☆☆☆☆☆

WEAKNESSES
DEFENSIVE CONTRIBUTION
BALL CONTROL

ROBERT
LEWANDOWSKI
90

PREFERRED FOOT
RIGHT

JERSEY NO.
9

PAC 75
DRI 87
SHO 91
DEF 44
PAS 80
PHY 84

TRANSFER HISTORY AND MARKET VALUE

800K Z. PRUSZKÓW 2008
1,4M LECH POZNAŃ 2010
50M B.DORTMUND 2014
45M BAYERN MUNICH 2022
15M BARCELONA 2024

POSITION

ROBERT LEWANDOWSKI

NEVER GIVE UP!

At just five years old, Robert Lewandowski had to play on teams with older boys because there were no soccer schools for kids his age in his area. But his passion for soccer was too strong to give up. Robert Lewandowski is an extraordinary soccer player born in Warsaw, Poland, on August 21, 1988.

From an early age, he loved soccer and began playing in the youth ranks of Legia Warsaw. His coach and first fan was his father, a physical education teacher. Unfortunately, during these years, Robert suffered a knee injury. His coaches were uncertain about his future; they thought he was too thin and frail, lacking the muscle needed to compete in championships. The team decided not to renew his contract, and Robert thought his career might end there.

However, Robert had a very supportive mother, a former volleyball player, who encouraged him to keep going. He eventually moved on to Borussia Dortmund. The beginning was not easy Lewa often found himself on the bench but he soon provided his talent to the coach. Earning the number 9 jersey, he scored an impressive 30 goals in his first season.

During his time at Dortmund, Lewandowski won two German championships and a domestic cup. In 2014, he transferred to Bayern Munich, where he continued to score prolifically, winning eight consecutive championships, four domestic cups, and a Champions League.

Robert is also the captain of the Polish national team, with whom he has participated in two European Championships and two World Cups.

He is the team's all-time top scorer with 132 goals in 138 games. He has won numerous awards, including Bundesliga top scorer seven times and FIFA Best Men's Player two years in a row.

Robert is an incredible striker, known for his scoring ability and for helping his teammates. He is a true champion who inspires children and young people around the world.

ROBERT LEWANDOWSKI
LEWANDOSKI'S ACCOMPLISHMENTS

Robert switched teams from Borussia Dortmund to Bayern Munich in the summer of 2014. During the second game of the 2014/15 season against FC Schalke 04, Sebastian Rode passed him the ball, and he scored without hesitation. It happened in the 10th minute of the match, and since then, he has scored an impressive 344 goals for his Munich team.

He has won the DFB-Pokal (German Cup) and a UEFA Champions League, contributing 15 goals during the tournament.

In the 2019/20 season, Robert Lewandowski scored a total of 55 goals in all competitions. During that season, he won the Bundesliga with Bayern Munich, scoring 34 goals in the German league.

Robert Lewandowski set a new record for the most goals scored in a single Bundesliga season by netting 41 goals in the 2020–21 season.

Robert won the FIFA Best Men's Player award two years in a row, in 2020 and 2021.

ROBERT LEWANDOWSKI
FIVE GOALS IN LESS THAN 9 MINUTES

Robert Lewandowski did something unforgettable in a match between Bayern Munich and Wolfsburg. He scored an incredible five goals in just under nine minutes.

It all started when Bayern coach Pep Guardiola decided to bring Lewandowski on in the second half. The game wasn't going well, and Lewandowski was brought in to make a difference. In no time, he scored the first goal, then the second, the third, the fourth, and finally the fifth! The entire stadium was in shock and amazement, hardly able to believe what they were witnessing.

At the end of the game, his teammates hugged each other, and everyone, even the coach, was in disbelief. Lewandowski high-fived the audience, overjoyed with his fantastic achievement!

ROBERT LEWANDOWSKI

Robert Lewandowski has scored a goal in the Bundesliga every 78 minutes! It's as if he scores a goal every time you watch an episode of your favorite cartoon.

When Robert plays soccer, everyone watches and cheers because he is so strong and fast! People often call him "LewanGOALski."

The passion for soccer was passed on to Robert by his father, a former physical education teacher. Both of his parents were athletes and always his number one fans.

Lewandowski has won the Polish Footballer of the Year award eleven times and has also been awarded Polish Sports Personality of the Year three times.

Robert Lewandowski is nicknamed "The Body" because of his impressive strength and fitness. This nickname was given to him by his friend and former teammate, Nuri Sahin when they played together at Dortmund.

PLAYER VALUE
$187M

NATIONALITY
BRA

JULY 12, 2000
23 YEARS

HEIGHT
5'7"

PREFERRED FOOT
RIGHT

STRENGTHS
DEEP-LYING PLAYMAKER
POSITIONING SENSE
LONG BALLS

SKILL MOVES
☆☆☆☆☆

WEAK FOOT
☆☆☆☆☆

WEAKNESSES
BALL CONTROL

JERSEY NO.
7

JÚNIOR VINÍCIUS
89

PAC 95

DRI 90

SHO 82

DEF 29

PAS 78

PHY 68

TRANSFER HISTORY AND MARKET VALUE

35M FLAMENGO 2018

180M REAL MADRID 2024

POSITION

VINÍCIUS JÚNIOR

THE BRAZILIAN OUTFIELDER

Vinicius Junior, born July 12, 2000, in São Gonçalo, Rio de Janeiro, was a young boy who loved playing soccer with his three siblings Lucas, Sophia, and Erika. They played on the streets and soccer fields of their neighborhood, and it quickly became clear that Vinicius had a special talent for the game.

From a young age, he was so skilled that everyone considered him a star of the future. The managers of Flamengo, one of Brazil's most famous clubs, noticed his talent early on and didn't waste the opportunity. They immediately included him in their youth team, knowing they had found a gem.

Even as a young boy, Vinicius was capable of winning many tournaments. He was incredibly fast, kept the ball always close to his feet, and never backed down from a challenge. It was no surprise that when he was only 17 years old, he was called up by Real Madrid.

During his time with the team, Vinicius scored crucial goals in the UEFA Champions League, helping Real Madrid win the trophy twice by 2024. In the 2021–22 season, he contributed three vital goals to the team's victory. In 2023–24, he added six more goals to his tally, including a decisive one in the final against Borussia Dortmund, proving his ability to shine in the most critical moments of Europe's most prestigious tournament.

Despite his youth, Vinicius has already won numerous awards and continues to improve every day. And you know what's great? Even now, as a famous soccer star, he never misses a chance to play with his three siblings.

VINÍCIUS JÚNIOR

JUNIOR'S ACCOMPLISHMENTS

In a crucial Champions League semifinal match between Real Madrid and Bayern Munich, Toni Kroos, one of Real Madrid's best players, saw Vinicius Junior free in front of Bayern's goal. With a perfect pass, Kroos set up Vinicius, who scored a fantastic goal that sent Real Madrid fans into a frenzy and put the team ahead.

To date, Vinicius has scored 83 goals for Real Madrid!

Vinicius Junior scored a hat trick in a very special match for Real Madrid on May 12, 2021, helping the team win the Spanish Super Cup.

In a Spanish league game against Levante, Vinicius played exceptionally well, scoring three goals and providing one assist in a 6–0 victory.

Vinicius Junior has won prestigious awards, such as Best Youth in the Champions League, and has lifted the La Liga title, the Champions League, and the FIFA Club World Cup twice with Real Madrid.

VINÍCIUS JÚNIOR

THE DECISIVE GOAL

In the UEFA Champions League final, Real Madrid, led by the electrifying talent of Vinicius Junior, faced Liverpool.

Wearing the 20, Vinicius was in top form. Real Madrid coach, Carlo Ancelotti, was counting on him to make a difference in this crucial match.

The first half ended in a 0–0 tie, with Liverpool pressing hard, but Real Madrid's defense held strong. Then, in the second half, a memorable moment occurred: in the 75th minute, after a quick counterattack by Real Madrid, the ball reached Vinicius on the left side of the field.

Vinicius elegantly dribbled past a defender, then accelerated toward the Liverpool penalty area. With a delicate touch, he placed the ball past the diving goalkeeper, Manuel Neuer, who couldn't stop Vinicius' precise shot. Real Madrid exploded with joy as Vinicius celebrated with his teammates. The score was 1–0 in favor of Real Madrid.

Liverpool fought desperately to equalize, but Real Madrid's well-organized defense held firm until the final whistle. Vinicius' goal secured Real Madrid's Champions League victory.

VINÍCIUS JÚNIOR

Vinicius started playing soccer at a very young age—only six years old! He began his journey with Flamengo, a very famous club in Brazil.

Do you know what Vinicius' favorite movie is? It's Karate Kid, a story about a boy who learns martial arts with the help of a wise master. Have you seen it?

Vinicius greatly admires a soccer idol. Do you know who it is? It's Neymar! We're sure you know who he is.

In 2020, Vinicius became the youngest player in history to score in "El Clásico" with his goal against Barcelona.

Vinicius created something special called the "Vini Jr. Institute," which helps kids learn new things using soccer! He also donated phones to his old school to help students learn better.

PLAYER VALUE
$21M

NATIONALITY
ARG

NOV 15, 1993
30 YEARS

HEIGHT
5'81"

PREFERRED FOOT
LEFT

STRENGTHS
PENALTY TAKER
DIRECT FREE KICKS
LONG BALLS

SKILL MOVES
★★★★☆

WEAK FOOT
★★★☆☆

WEAKNESSES
BALL CONTROL

JERSEY NO.
21

PAULO DYBALA 86

PAC 80	DRI 90
SHO 85	DEF 40
PAS 85	PHY 60

TRANSFER HISTORY AND MARKET VALUE

- **2M** INSTITUTO CÓRDOBA 2011
- **23M** PALERMO 2015
- **35M** JUVENTUS 2022
- **20M** ROMA 2024

POSITION

ST
AM

PAULO DYBALA

FROM ARGENTINA TO ITALY, MAKING DREAMS COME TRUE

Paulo Dybala loved playing soccer more than anything else in the world. He grew up in a small town in Argentina called Laguna Larga, dreaming of becoming a professional soccer player.

He dribbled past everyone, scored countless goals, and inspired his friends with his skills. At the age of 10, he tried out for a big team, Newell's Old Boys, but unfortunately, they didn't take him. However, that setback didn't stop him.

He continued training with his small team, Instituto, where he kept scoring goals. At 17, his dream finally came true when he signed his first professional contract with the team.

Dybala played two years with Instituto, scoring many goals and attracting the attention of major European clubs. In 2012, at just 19 years old, he moved to Italy to play for Palermo. It was a big change he was far from his family and friends, didn't speak the language, and Italian soccer was very different from Argentine soccer.

But Paulo was strong and determined. He worked hard, learned the language, and soon started scoring goals even in Serie A. In 2015, after three successful years at Palermo, he moved to Juventus, one of Italy's biggest teams.

With Juventus, Paulo Dybala won five Scudetti, four Italian Cups, and three Italian Super Cups, totaling twelve trophies in seven years. He also played in a UEFA Champions League final in 2017.

Besides team successes, Dybala has earned individual honors as Serie A MVP in 2019–20, being named twice in the Serie A Team of the Year and once in the UEFA Champions League Team of the Year. His contributions have been crucial to Juventus' recent successes.

Paulo Dybala is a talented, fast, and creative striker, capable of scoring goals in many different ways.

PAULO DYBALA
DYBALA'S ACCOMPLISHMENTS

At a young age, Paulo broke a record by becoming the youngest person to score in a professional game in Argentina, even surpassing a record held by Mario Kempes, a famous Argentine player from the 1970s.

In 2015, Paulo joined Juventus, one of Italy's strongest teams. In his first season with his new team, he scored an impressive 21 goals in all competitions. One of the highlights was when he scored against Lazio in the Italian Super Cup, helping Juventus secure the win.

In 2017, Paulo and Juventus faced Barcelona, a team with stars like Messi, Neymar, and Suarez. Paulo scored two incredible goals within the first 25 minutes.

On April 11, 2017, Paulo Dybala delivered an outstanding performance by scoring three goals against Barcelona in a Champions League match, playing a key role in Juventus' 3–0 victory over the Catalan giants.

Paulo Dybala scored his first hat trick in a Roma shirt during a crucial match against Torino, once again demonstrating his innate talent for scoring decisive goals. The match ended in a 3–2 victory for Roma, despite an own goal by Huijsen in the 88th minute, which was not enough to overturn the result.

PAULO DYBALA

AN ENVIABLE DEBUT

During the 2015 Italian Super Cup in Shanghai, China, Juventus faced Lazio in a very important match. Paulo Dybala was on the field, but everyone called him "La Joya," which means "The Jewel" in Spanish.

Paulo had just joined Juventus from Palermo, and everyone was eager to see what he could do with his new team. In the second half of the match, with the score still uncertain, Paulo entered the field with determination and grit. It didn't take long for him to showcase his talent. With a perfect pass from Paul Pogba, Paulo unleashed a powerful shot into the goal.

Juventus won that match 2–0, thanks in part to Paulo's goal. It was an incredible start to his adventure with the Bianconeri. From that day on, Paulo Dybala became one of the brightest stars in world soccer.

PAULO DYBALA

Paulo Dybala is good friends with Lionel Messi; they often hang out together and play friendly games.

Do you know what Paulo Dybala does when he scores a goal? He puts one hand in front of his mouth, with his thumb and forefinger outstretched, imitating a gladiator's mask. This gesture is his way of paying tribute to the heroes of the past.

After Paulo Dybala won the World Cup with Argentina, he found five missed calls from his coach, Josè Mourinho. Mourinho was so happy for him that he wanted to know if another player, Leandro Paredes, would come to play with them at Roma. Dybala confirmed that Paredes would join, making Mourinho very happy!

Paulo Dybala ha iniziato a giocare a calcio per un club argentino chiamato Instituto Atlético Central Córdoba quando era giovane, prima di trasferirsi in Italia per giocare con squadre come il Palermo e la Juventus.

Paulo Dybala began his soccer career at Instituto Atlético Central Córdoba in Argentina before moving to Italy to play for teams like Palermo and Juventus.

PLAYER VALUE

$77,5M

NATIONALITY

FRA

JUNE 23, 1972

52 YEARS

HEIGHT

6'07"

PREFERRED FOOT

BOTH

STRENGTHS

BALL CONTROL

DIRECT FREE KICKS

LONG BALLS

SKILL MOVES

☆☆☆☆☆

WEAK FOOT

☆☆☆☆⯪

WEAKNESSES

TEMPERAMENT

JERSEY NO.

5

ZINEDINE

ZIDANE

96

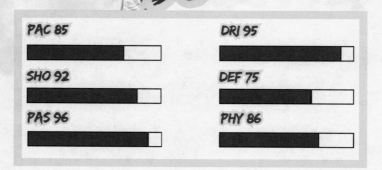

PAC 85

SHO 92

PAS 96

DRI 95

DEF 75

PHY 86

TRANSFER HISTORY AND MARKET VALUE

POSITION

2M AS CANNES 1990

7M BORDEAUX 1992

3,5M JUVENTUS 1996

77,5M REAL MADRID 2001

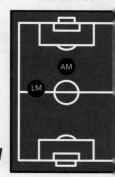

ZINEDINE ZIDANE
ZIZOU OF MARSEILLE

Zinédine Zidane, affectionately known as "Zizou," was born in Marseille, France. His father, Smail, came from Algeria and worked in France as a bricklayer. Zidane met his future wife, Véronique, when he was 17, and they married in 1994. They have four sons—Enzo, Luca, Théo, and Elyaz—who all play soccer, just like their father!

Zidane was passionate about sports, particularly soccer and judo, but soccer was his true love. At age nine, he joined the neighborhood club, AS Forest 11, where he quickly became the captain. In 1982, he joined Saint-Henri and the following year moved on to Septèmes-les-Vallons.

In 1986, during a selection process, he caught the eye of Jean Varraud, a scout from Cannes, who brought him to the French Riviera for a six-week tryout. The tryout ended with Zidane signing his first professional contract.

At age 15, Zidane joined the Cannes team under the guidance of coach Guy Lacombe. When Cannes was relegated, he moved to Bordeaux, where coach Rolland Courbis affectionately nicknamed him "Zizou." Alongside his friends Dugarry and Bixente Lizarazu, they formed the famous "Bordeaux Triangle." Zizou scored 10 goals in his first season and helped Bordeaux qualify for the UEFA Cup.

In 1996, Zidane transferred to Juventus, where he initially faced some challenges but soon became a star. With Juventus, he won the Intercontinental Cup, the UEFA Super Cup, and two Serie A titles.

In 1998, Zidane won the Ballon d'Or. In 2001, Zidane moved to Real Madrid for a record fee, and with Real Madrid, he scored an incredible volley in the Champions League final against Bayer Leverkusen, securing victory for his team. In 2003, Zidane won the Spanish championship and scored nine goals that season.

Zidane also had a remarkable career with the French national team. In 1998, he led France to World Cup glory, scoring two goals in the final against Brazil. In 2000, he added a European championship to his list of accomplishments. Zidane retired from playing soccer in 2006, following the infamous headbutt incident in the World Cup final against Italy.

As a coach, Zidane led Real Madrid to three consecutive Champions League titles, an extraordinary feat. He retired from coaching in 2018 but remains an iconic figure in world soccer.

ZINEDINE ZIDANE
ZIDANE'S ACCOMPLISHMENTS

Zidane scored an impressive 156 goals in his career, playing in 798 games. This means that, on average, he scored at least one goal every five games.

After leading France to World Cup victory, Zidane received the prestigious Ballon d'Or in December 1998, becoming the fourth French player to win this coveted trophy.

In 1997, Zidane played a brilliant match against Ajax for Juventus, providing two beautiful assists and scoring a magical goal to help Juve win 3–1.

In 2002, Zidane scored an unforgettable volley for Real Madrid in the Champions League final against Bayer Leverkusen. With the score tied at 1–1, he struck the ball with his left foot, sending it into the top corner. Real Madrid won 2–1, and some journalists still consider it one of the most beautiful goals in Champions League history.

When Zidane started at Juventus, he initially played in a deeper role but soon moved forward, where he showcased his extraordinary talent. In 1996, he won the Intercontinental Cup, the Super Cup, and the Serie A title. After winning the World Cup with France in 1998, he was awarded the Ballon d'Or and named FIFA World Player of the Year.

ZINEDINE ZIDANE

A MEMORABLE WORLD CHAMPIONSHIP, BEYOND THE HEADBUT ON MATERAZZI

Despite Zidane's brilliance on the field, many remember him for the infamous headbutt during the 2006 World Cup final against Italy. Zidane was exhausted, worried about his mother's health, and frustrated with the progress of the match. After a brief altercation with Marco Materazzi, Zidane reacted by headbutting him in the chest.

The referee immediately punished the gesture with a red card. Despite this, Zidane's World Cup performance was so outstanding that he won the Golden Ball as the tournament's best player.

During the group stage, France drew 0–0 with Switzerland and 1–1 with South Korea.
Zidane did not play in the 2–0 victory against Togo, which secured France's qualification for the round of 16. Against Spain, Zidane provided an assist and scored a goal, leading France to a 3–1 victory. In the quarterfinals against Brazil, Zidane delivered a masterful performance with perfect passes and spectacular dribbling, guiding France to a 1-0 win.
In the semifinal against Portugal, Zidane scored the only goal from a penalty kick, ensuring France's place in the final.

In the final against Italy, Zidane scored a magnificent penalty before being sent off during extra time for his headbutt on Materazzi. France ultimately lost on penalties, but Zidane was still awarded the tournament's best player, highlighting his greatness until the end of his career.

ZINEDINE ZIDANE

When Zidane was playing for Bordeaux, an English team, Blackburn Rovers showed interest in signing him. However, the club's manager famously said, "Why take Zidane when we already have Tim Sherwood?" Blackburn missed the chance to sign one of the greatest footballers in history.

When Zidane arrived at Juventus, he revealed that, as a child, he had supported Juventus in Italy and Barcelona in Spain.

Zidane is multilingual, speaking French, Italian, English, Spanish, and Berber, the language of his Algerian heritage.

When Zidane was young and played for Cannes, he once hit an opponent who mocked his origins. As punishment, he was required to clean the club's premises.

Zidane is widely regarded as one of the greatest soccer players of all time. The BBC named him the best European player ever, and FIFA recognized him as the best player of the past 50 years.

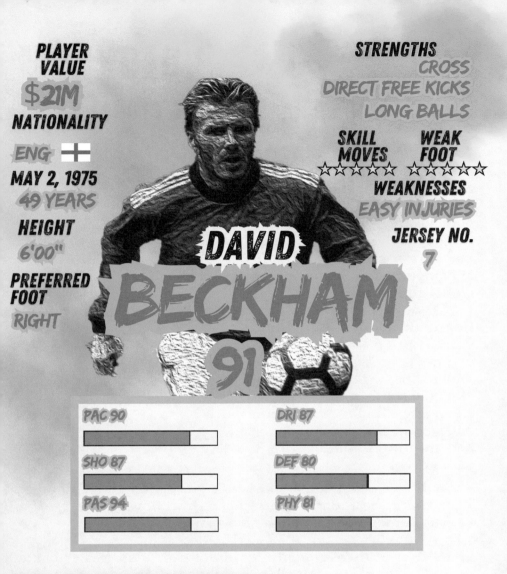

PLAYER VALUE

$21M

NATIONALITY

ENG

MAY 2, 1975

49 YEARS

HEIGHT

6'00"

PREFERRED FOOT

RIGHT

STRENGTHS

CROSS

DIRECT FREE KICKS

LONG BALLS

SKILL MOVES
☆☆☆☆☆

WEAK FOOT
☆☆☆☆☆

WEAKNESSES

EASY INJURIES

JERSEY NO.

7

DAVID

BECKHAM

91

PAC 90

DRI 87

SHO 87

DEF 80

PAS 94

PHY 81

TRANSFER HISTORY AND MARKET VALUE

9M MANCHESTER UNITED 1993

37,5M REAL MADRID 2003

20M L.A GALAXY 2007

15M MILAN 2009

5M PSG 2013

POSITION

DAVID BECKHAM

THE AMBASSADOR OF GLOBAL SOCCER

As a child, David Beckham always went to the stadium with his dad to watch Manchester United games. Although he was already playing soccer, he never imagined he would become a global superstar.

Beckham showed his talent early on, playing for his county team, Essex. In the mid-1980s, he went to Manchester to train with the legendary Bobby Charlton, and at just 11 years old, he had the opportunity to train with Barcelona.

Though he was initially passed over by Leyton Orient and Tottenham, he found success with Brimsdown Rovers, where he was named the best Under-15 player in 1990.

In 1991, Beckham signed a contract with Manchester United. In the 1994–95 season, he was loaned to Preston North End, where he scored two goals in five games. Upon returning to Manchester United, he played a key role in helping the team win the Premier League, the FA Cup in 1995–96, and the Champions League in 1999, contributing crucial corner kicks in the final!

In 2003, Beckham moved to Real Madrid, where he won La Liga and a Spanish Super Cup. In 2007, he joined the Los Angeles Galaxy, where he helped grow Major League Soccer and won two MLS Cups.

In 2013, Beckham played for Paris Saint-Germain, winning the French championship and donating his salary to charity. With the England national team, he played in three World Cups and two European Championships.

DAVID BECKHAM
BECKHAM'S ACCOMPLISHMENTS

David Beckham scored a sensational goal against Wimbledon in 1996 by kicking the ball in from halfway across the field! His shot soared over goalkeeper Neil Sullivan, sending the crowd into a frenzy. This goal has become one of the most famous in Premier League history.

In the 1999 Champions League final, Manchester United was trailing, but Beckham delivered two perfect corner kicks that led to two goals in the final minutes! Thanks to him, Manchester United secured the victory.

In 2001, during a crucial World Cup qualifying match, Beckham scored a last-minute free kick, ensuring England's place in the 2002 tournament.

In 2013, Beckham helped Paris Saint-Germain win France's Ligue 1 championship. He received a standing ovation and was affectionately tossed in the air by his teammates in celebration.

In 2003, after a falling out with Sir Alex Ferguson, Beckham left Manchester United and moved to Real Madrid for £24.5 million, joining the Galácticos. Over 4 seasons, Beckham played 159 games, made 52 assists, and scored 20 goals, winning La Liga and the Spanish Super Cup. In 2007, he moved to the LA Galaxy and secured the option to own a team, which later became Inter Miami.

DAVID BECKHAM

BECKHAM'S REVENGE

The stage was set: England vs. Argentina in the 2002 World Cup. On the field was David Beckham, determined to give his best. Two years earlier, during the 1998 World Cup in France, Beckham had experienced a low point he was sent off, and Argentina eliminated England. It was a difficult and sad time for Beckham.

Now, it was time for redemption. England was awarded a penalty, and Beckham had the chance to make amends. With immense determination and courage, he stepped up to the ball, fully aware of the pressure on his shoulders.

He struck the ball with precision, sending it straight into the net, past the Argentine goalkeeper. Beckham celebrated with pure joy as English fans erupted in celebration.

This goal was significant not only because it gave England the lead but also because it symbolized Beckham's redemption. He had overcome the pain of the past and led England forward in the World Cup. It was a moment of immense happiness and satisfaction for Beckham.

DAVID BECKHAM

David Beckham has the number 99 tattooed on his little finger, representing the magical year when he won numerous trophies, got married, and had a child.

In 2005, Beckham played a key role in helping London secure the 2012 Olympics! On the big day, he rode a speedboat down the River Thames, proudly carrying the Olympic torch with a big smile on his face.

In September 2022, following the death of Queen Elizabeth II, Beckham lined up with the public to pay his respects. He waited over 13 hours, just like everyone else. Despite his fame, Beckham chose not to skip the line, and many applauded him for his gesture of respect and humility.

When Beckham joined Real Madrid, he chose the number 23 for his jersey, a nod to his admiration for basketball legend Michael Jordan.

David Beckham became the first Briton to play 100 games in the Champions League.

PLAYER VALUE
$21M

NATIONALITY
ARG

OCT 30, 1960
DECEASED

HEIGHT
5'38"

STRENGTHS
DRIBBLING
SET PIECES
LEADERSHIP

SKILL MOVES
★★★★☆

WEAK FOOT
★★★★★

WEAKNESSES
TEMPERAMENT

DIEGO ARMANDO
MARADONA
98

PREFERRED FOOT
LEFT

JERSEY NO.
21

PAC 94	DRI 98
SHO 95	DEF 43
PAS 93	PHY 79

TRANSFER HISTORY AND MARKET VALUE

Value	Club	Year
3,8M	AGERTINOS	1981
3,8M	BOCA JUNIORS	1982
LOAN	BARCELONA	1984
7,3M	NAPOLI	1991
6,9M	SEVILLA	1993
5M	NEWELL'S	1994
3M	BOCA JUNIORS	1995

POSITION

DIEGO ARMANDO MARADONA

THE GOLDEN BOY

Diego Armando Maradona was born on October 30, 1960, in Argentina, and from a very young age he was already a soccer star! Growing up with five sisters and two brothers who all loved to play soccer, Diego quickly developed a passion for the game. He played for the "Cebollitas" team as a child, and it was clear to everyone that he had a special talent.

Maradona was a magician on the field. His dribbling skills were so extraordinary that it seemed like the ball was glued to his foot!

Although he wasn't very tall, Diego had strong legs and incredible balance, which helped him glide past opponents effortlessly.

Throughout his career, Maradona played for many fantastic teams. He became a champion at a young age with Argentinos Juniors. He then moved to Boca Juniors, helping the team win the 1981 Apertura Metropolitano Championship. While at Barcelona, he won the King's Cup and the Copa de La Liga, despite facing some injuries.

However, the real magic happened when he joined Napoli. There, he transformed the team into one of the best in Italy and Europe, winning the Scudetto (Serie A Championship) in 1986–87, the Coppa Italia in the 1986-87 season, the UEFA Cup in the 1988–89 season, and the Italian Super Cup in 1990, triumphing over Juventus.

Maradona also made history with the Argentine national team.

He achieved incredible feats in the World Cup, leading Argentina to victory in 1986 and scoring two of the most famous goals in soccer history: the "Goal of the Century" and the iconic "Hand of God."

Despite facing some difficult times, Diego Maradona remained a true lover of soccer and his family. He is remembered as one of the greatest soccer players of all time, and his story teaches us that with passion and determination, dreams can come true!

DIEGO ARMANDO MARADONA

MARADONA'S ACCOMPLISHMENTS

When Diego Maradona was just 15 years old, on October 20, 1976, he made his debut with Argentinos Juniors. Although the team lost 1–0 in that first game, Maradona made a lasting impression with a spectacular nutmeg over an opponent. During his time with the team, he scored an incredible 100 goals.

In 1983, while playing for Barcelona against Real Madrid during El Clasico, Maradona dribbled past the goalkeeper and paused before scoring, leaving the defender frozen in place. This move was so extraordinary that the crowd at the Bernabéu, Real Madrid's home ground, gave Maradona a standing ovation.

In 1986, Diego led Argentina to World Cup glory in Mexico. On June 22, during the match against England, Maradona scored two unforgettable goals: one with the "Hand of God" and the other dazzling run through the English defense, known as the "Goal of the Century."

In 1987, Maradona guided Napoli to its first-ever Serie A championship. On May 10, Napoli secured the title by beating Fiorentina. The city erupted with celebration, turning into one big party in honor of Diego and his incredible achievement.

In 1990, during the World Cup, Argentina faced tough challenges, but Maradona had a plan. He played a crucial role in helping the team win key matches, including victories against Brazil and Italy.

DIEGO ARMANDO MARADONA

WHEN ALL SEEMS LOST ...

On March 29, 1989, Napoli faced a crucial UEFA Cup quarterfinal match against Juventus. The team was in a tough spot, having lost 2–0 in the previous game in Turin. But they didn't give up!

As the game began at the San Paolo Stadium, Maradona worked his magic! In the 10th minute, he scored a penalty, igniting the crowd with joy. Just before halftime, Andrea Carnevale added another goal, putting Napoli ahead 2–0.

The game continued, and it seemed Napoli would have to wait until the last moment for a decisive outcome. And, indeed, in the 119th minute, Alessandro Renica leaped and headed the ball into the net, securing a 3–0 victory for Napoli. The fans erupted in celebrations, thrilled by the dramatic comeback that sent Napoli to the semifinals!

DIEGO ARMANDO MARADONA

When Diego Maradona was an 11-year-old boy, he was so good at soccer that everyone watched in amazement. A reporter once made a mistake and wrote his name as "Caradona," but even with the funny name, Diego never disappointed on the field!

Once, a fan found strands of Maradona's hair on a seat of the soccer team's plane. He collected them and took them to a bar in Naples, where they are still on display today.

When Diego traveled abroad, he always wore two watches—one showing the local time and the other showing the time in Argentina, so he would always know what time it was back home.

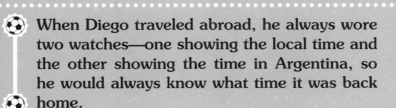

Maradona scored several goals with his hand during matches, the most famous being the "Hand of God" against England. Once, Zico, another famous player, tried to point out Maradona's handball to the referee, but to no avail!

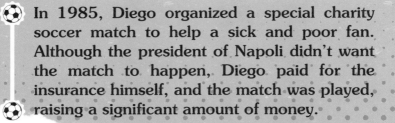

In 1985, Diego organized a special charity soccer match to help a sick and poor fan. Although the president of Napoli didn't want the match to happen, Diego paid for the insurance himself, and the match was played, raising a significant amount of money.

PLAYER VALUE

$21M

NATIONALITY

GER

SEP 11, 1945
DECEASED

HEIGHT
5'94"

STRENGTHS
GAME VISION
BALL CONTROL
LEADERSHIP

SKILL MOVES
☆☆☆☆☆

WEAK FOOT
☆☆☆☆☆

WEAKNESSES
EASY INJURIES

FRANZ BECKENBAUER

93

PREFERRED FOOT
RIGHT

JERSEY NO.
5

PAC 81

DRI 79

SHO 82

DEF 94

PAS 91

PHY 81

TRANSFER HISTORY AND MARKET VALUE

900K   BAYERN MUNICH 1977

400M   N.Y COSMOS 1980

200M   HAMBURG 1982

POSITION

FRANZ BECKENBAUER

THE CHARISMATIC KAISER

You may be too young to know this great soccer player, but it's important to talk about the legends who made soccer history. Franz Beckenbauer, known as "The Kaiser" because he was always the center of attention, was born in 1945 in Munich, Germany. He had an older brother named Walter and an uncle who played for Bayern Munich, just like him. Franz grew up in a close-knit family and, as a child, dreamed of becoming a great soccer player.

In the 1970s, Franz lived in a nice town called Grünwald and later moved to Switzerland and Austria. He was married three times and had five children, including a son who also became a soccer player but sadly passed away in 2015.

Franz played soccer for his favorite team, Bayern Munich, where he won many trophies, including two Ballon d'Or awards, as well as numerous national cups and championships.

When he was young, he was invited to play for Inter Milan, a team he never joined. Later in his career, he played for the New York Cosmos in the United States, where he won three North American championships in a row, before returning to Germany to play with Hamburg.

Franz was not only a great player but also a fantastic coach.

He led the German national team to win the World Cup in 1990. After his coaching career, he became an executive for major teams and an organizer of soccer events.

In the later years of his career, Franz faced some difficulties, but he is still remembered today as one of the most special and influential figures in soccer.

FRANZ BECKENBAUER

BECKENBAUER'S ACCOMPLISHMENTS

In 1974, Franz Beckenbauer captained West Germany to victory in the World Cup. Despite injuring his shoulder, he continued to play and helped his team secure the title.

In 1966, Beckenbauer played in the World Cup final against England, where he faced the famous Bobby Charlton. Although England won 4–2 after extra time, Beckenbauer's skill and tenacity in stopping opponents were on full display, making the match an iconic moment in his career.

Beckenbauer won two Ballon d'Or awards, one in 1972 and one in 1976. He was one of the few defenders to win this prestigious award, proving his exceptional talent and ranking among the best soccer players in the world.

Franz helped Bayern Munich win the European Champions Cup three times in a row, from 1974 to 1976. This was a remarkable achievement, as no other team had managed to win the cup so many times consecutively.

After returning to coach Bayern Munich in 1996, Beckenbauer led the team to victory in the UEFA Cup, further cementing his legacy.

FRANZ BECKENBAUER
AN UNMISTAKABLE STYLE

Franz Beckenbauer was playing for Bayern Munich in a memorable match against Real Madrid on April 14, 1976. It was a European Champions Cup semifinal, and Bayern Munich was aiming for a spot in the final.

Even though Beckenbauer played as a defender, he didn't just stop the opposing attackers. With his elegant and precise style, he made long, spectacular passes that got past all the Real Madrid defenders. He often used the outside of his foot to strike the ball, creating a curved trajectory that was difficult to predict.

Throughout the match, Beckenbauer demonstrated his incredible skills. His brilliant passes helped his teammates create numerous scoring opportunities. In the end, Bayern Munich won 2–0. That victory was pivotal, as Bayern went on to win the Champions Cup for the third consecutive time, thanks in part to Beckenbauer's brilliance.

This match is remembered as one of Beckenbauer's best, showcasing his talent and how his innovative style of play could make a difference at crucial moments.

CURIOSITY ABOUT BECKENBAUER

FRANZ BECKENBAUER

Beckenbauer is one of the few people to have won the World Cup both as a player and as a coach.

When he played for the New York Cosmos, Beckenbauer had the opportunity to play alongside Pele, another legendary soccer player.

Beckenbauer received an offer to make a film about his life, but he declined, preferring that his story remain in people's memory rather than on the screen.

As a young player, Beckenbauer was supposed to move to play in Italy with Inter Milan, but the deal fell through. His dream of playing in the San Siro stadium was never realized, especially after Italy's failure in the 1966 World Cup led to a temporary ban on purchasing foreign players.

Franz Beckenbauer was the first player to win the Bundesliga with Bayern Munich three times in a row.

LAMINE YAMAL 81

PLAYER VALUE
$129M

NATIONALITY
SPA

JULY 13, 2007
17 YEARS

HEIGHT
5'91"

PREFERRED FOOT
LEFT

STRENGTHS
PASSES
CONTINUITY
HIGH PRESSING

SKILL MOVES
★★★★

WEAK FOOT
★★★

WEAKNESSES
DEFENSIVE PHASE

JERSEY NO.
27

PAC 69

SHO 73

PAS 73

DRI 82

DEF 25

PHY 61

TRANSFER HISTORY AND MARKET VALUE

0M BARCELONA B 2015

129M BARCELONA 2024

POSITION

LAMINE YAMAL
VERY YOUNG YET TALENTED

Lamine Yamal is proof that even at a very young age, you can accomplish heroic feats.

This young soccer prodigy was born in 2007 in Esplugues de Llobregat, Spain, making him just 17 years old today. From a very young age, he had a deep passion for soccer and spent every spare moment playing with a ball. He dreamed of becoming a great soccer player like Lionel Messi.

When he was only five years old, Lamine began playing seriously for the local Rocafonda team. His talent was so obvious that he soon moved to Barcelona to join FC Barcelona's renowned youth academy, La Masia. Despite his young age, Lamine quickly demonstrated exceptional skill in dribbling and scoring goals.

At age seven, he participated in the "League of Promises" tournament, where he scored seven goals and was voted the tournament's best player. Although his team did not win, Lamine had already caught everyone's attention with his talent.

In 2023, at just 15 years old, Lamine made his debut with Barcelona's first team, becoming the fifth youngest player to play in the Spanish La Liga. He continued to impress by scoring his first goal in La Liga at age 16, breaking the record for Barcelona's youngest goal scorer. He also scored in the Supercopa and Copa del Rey, proving that he is a true soccer star in the making. With his extraordinary talent and dedication, Lamine Yamal has already become a great promise in soccer, showing the world that even the youngest can achieve incredible results with passion and commitment.

LAMINE YAMAL
YAMAL'S ACCOMPLISHMENTS

- With FC Barcelona, Lamine played fifty-five games, scored eight goals, and made eight assists. He had only six yellow cards and no red cards.

- With the Spanish national team, he played fourteen games, scored three goals, and made seven assists. For the Under-17 team, he played five games, scored four goals, and made two assists.

- Lamine Yamal participated in UEFA EURO 2024 when he was only 16 years and 338 days old, making him the youngest player ever to take part in this major soccer tournament.

- Lamine won the EURO 2024 final with Spain—just one day after turning 17 years old.

- At just 16 years and 57 days old, Lamine scored a goal during a qualifying match for the EURO tournament against Georgia, becoming the youngest ever scorer in the qualifiers for this important tournament, demonstrating his great talent from a young age.

LAMINE YAMAL

UEFA 2024'S BEST GOAL

During the semi-final of EURO 2024, Spain faced off against France. The French were leading 1–0, but then came Lamine's magic moment!

In the 21st minute, with the game still in the balance, Yamal took the ball outside the box and did something incredible. He performed a series of feints with the ball, then struck it with his left foot, sending it right under the crossbar. The goal was so spectacular that everyone was amazed! With that goal, he became the youngest ever scorer in the history of the UEFA EURO.

Spain later scored another goal and won the match 2–1. Thanks to Yamal and his team, Spain advanced to the final! This special goal by Yamal was chosen as the best of the tournament by the coaches.

CURIOSITIES ABOUT YAMAL

LAMINE YAMAL

Lamine Yamal was born in 2007 and, at just 15 years and 290 days old, became the youngest player in Barcelona's history to make his league debut.

Yamal is of Moroccan descent and also has citizenship from Equatorial Guinea.

Yamal is often compared to Lionel Messi because, like Messi, he is left-footed and received his first first-team call-up at age 15.

Barcelona coach Xavi praises Yamal for his boldness and potential, suggesting that he could be immediately useful to the team. Patrick Kluivert, former striker and youth manager, describes Yamal as having "the complete package," with skills that cover everything needed to be a great soccer player.

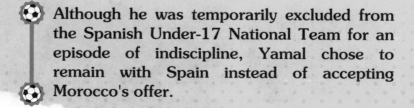

Although he was temporarily excluded from the Spanish Under-17 National Team for an episode of indiscipline, Yamal chose to remain with Spain instead of accepting Morocco's offer.

THANKS FOR READING!

Dear reader,
we hope these stories have inspired you and given you the confidence to believe in yourself and chase your dreams.

Remember, with hard work and determination, any dream can come true.

But the adventure doesn't end here... We've prepared even more exciting content for you!

- 50+ Printable Coloring Pages
- 3 Sneak Peeks of Other RookieLand Books
- Parenting Tips
- Fun Family Recipes and Activities
- Exclusive Facebook Group with giveaways for more outstanding books

Scan the QR CODE below to access these gifts and get exclusive previews of our upcoming releases.

It only takes a few seconds!

Thank you again for choosing us...

If you enjoyed the content, leave a positive review or write to us privately if you have any suggestions for improvement:

rookielandbooks@gmail.com

We hope to see you again soon!

Made in the USA
Columbia, SC
14 December 2024